UNLOCKING

Potential

UNLOCKING

Potential

Organizing a School Inside a Prison

HILDERBRAND PELZER III

Outskirts Press, Inc.
Denver, Colorado

Unlocking Potential
Organizing a School Inside a Prison
All Rights Reserved.
Copyright © 2011 Hilderbrand Pelzer III
v4.0 r1.0

Cover Photo © 2017 thinkstockphotos.com.
All rights reserved - used with permission.

Outskirts Press, Inc.
http://www.outskirtspress.com

ISBN: 978-1-4327-7027-3

Outskirts Press and the "OP" logo are trademarks belonging to
Outskirts Press, Inc.

PRINTED IN THE UNITED STATES OF AMERICA

Contents

Foreword by Carolyn E. Paige

I HAD NEVER given much thought to correctional education, nor had I known people who were incarcerated, even though I grew up in an impoverished neighborhood. My family was intact and I received immeasurable support from my parents, extended family, and a few great teachers. For me, as for many urban youths, temptation was always around the corner; but my parents constantly reinforced their belief in the five children in our family. We belonged to them and we knew right from wrong. Their expectations were always front and center.

As a young adult and recent college graduate, I went to work for the School District of Philadelphia as a high school English teacher. I worked with many young people of various ethnicities who were growing up in circumstances like my own; and, as their teacher, I worked diligently and encouraged them to gain as much education as possible. My greatest understanding came when I acknowledged this to myself: "They, my students, can because they think they can." I have always believed that learning is everything, and I shared this belief with my students time after time, always followed by a healthy dose of encouragement: "I know you can do it"; "Start studying earlier next time"; or "Come to my classroom after school; I'll wait for you!"

Because my parents believed in my siblings and me, my teachers supported us, and we believed in ourselves. I, in turn, believed in my students. I recognize that educators have enormous power over students in classrooms—the power to encourage or crush their aspirations. I have come to believe that true educators must commit themselves to giving students the support they need to acquire an education that will sustain them and assure each of them a better future. Failure is not an option! If we believe we are the gatekeepers of our society, we must remember that "they can because they think they can"—helping them to *believe* they can is our duty as educators.

I worked as an English teacher for nearly twenty-three years. Aside from my daily classes, I was a drama coach, a Flag Corps coordinator, and a teacher of English in evening high schools for adults, the latter for almost twenty-two years. I gained great insight into students and the ability to assess the kinds of support they need to be successful. I came to understand that all people deserve the opportunity to become their personal best. The development of each individual to his or her greatest potential leads to a better informed public that is able to achieve emotional and intellectual satisfaction in life.

Often, an adult student in my evening classes asked me to help write a resume or recommendation letter for potential employment. It wasn't a burden for me. I considered it an honor because these adults sought me out to support them and trusted me to do so. I arrived early to class to give students a chance to make such requests. Recently, I saw one of my adult students at a local restaurant. She informed me that she remembered our many conversations and my urging her to encourage her children to seek higher education. She announced proudly that both of her children were enrolled in local colleges. I gave her a broad smile and embraced her. Then, I reminded her of my favorite saying, "They can because they think they can!"

Even though I had worked with students from many backgrounds, it wasn't until I went to work with Principal Hilderbrand Pelzer III at the Pennypack House School in the Philadelphia Prison System that I became acutely aware of how many truly bright young men with inadequate educations were incarcerated. Pennypack is a public high school in the School District of Philadelphia, located within the Philadelphia Prison System.

The Philadelphia Prison System is located in the northeast corner of the city and is the fifth-largest urban county jail system in the United States. The city has one of the highest incarceration rates in the country. With a daily census of over 9000 inmates, the Philadelphia Prison System operates and manages six major correctional institutions on the grounds of a correctional complex. Housed in adult facilities, you will find a population of direct-file/certified juveniles—incarcerated school-age youth who, because they have been arraigned or convicted of serious crimes, bypass the usual filings and proceedings in family or juvenile courts and are sent straight to adult criminal courts and sentencing.

At Pennypack, I met boys as young as fourteen, mere children. Although some of their crimes were very serious, they laughed and played like the young children they were. Even though the system punished them as adults, I saw that they were still children—children we had failed by not teaching and not protecting them from circumstances that would destroy their lives.

I had worked with fifteen school principals during my thirty-two-year career in the Philadelphia schools; but, I found Principal Pelzer exceptional. He was innovative, a great listener, and willing to embrace, help, and encourage the young men incarcerated in the Philadelphia Prison System. He was a consummate professional.

I would often accompany him to the prison's housing units to visit with the boys and encourage them to think about their education. On occasion, I would go to the housing units alone and bring boys books to read while they were being held in protective custody. Through observation and listening, I realized that some boys had never had a relationship with a man who sat and talked with them, discussed their fears, and helped them to understand the tragic decisions that had led them to prison. In the midst of all that, Principal Pelzer continually encouraged the boys to learn.

In the course of his work, he proved that students in the prison system would respond to good instruction and could become successful learners. He aligned courses using Pennsylvania state standards and used the standards to propel students with academic abilities into more challenging courses. Students needing additional academic support were given opportunities to take concentrated skill-building courses.

On numerous occasions, visitors to Pennypack House School observed good instruction and saw students engaged in learning and enjoying it. A few examples are: researched-based literacy and math programs, classroom libraries, computers and other technology tools in the classrooms, and lively classroom environments. With the support of prison officials and corrections officers, we held a science fair to show work done by our incarcerated juvenile inmates. Officials and officers participated by voting on the best projects. As officials circulated from table to table, students answered questions about their projects and described in detail their experimental approach and research. On other occasions, graduating seniors had completed senior projects and presented their work to a broad audience. The principal, administrative assistant, prison officials, officers, teachers, and juvenile inmates participated in evaluating the projects. Senior projects included PowerPoint presentations, tri fold standing boards, and addresses to the group, in which the seniors presented their research.

Not all incarcerated youths remain in jail; some are found innocent and are returned to their communities. Depending on the length of their incarceration, some youths may return home more knowledgeable and more confident of their abilities if they are able to study and learn during their time in jail or prison. It is crucial that we provide all direct-file/certified young people with both encouragement and the academic tools and skills they need to become productive citizens.

For those school-age youths who will be incarcerated for long terms, acquiring an education will broaden their experiences and enable them to focus on bettering themselves while incarcerated. When these juvenile inmates are involved in constructive learning, they are less likely to engage in antisocial and violent acts. Becoming knowledgeable about their world gives them a bridge to constructive thinking.

Correctional education benefits society and provides solutions for improving student achievement in challenging learning environments. It also helps to quell unrest behind bars, leading to a safer environment for both the incarcerated and the staff.

Acknowledgments

I WOULD NOT have undertaken this manuscript without the encouragement of a close family friend, Bernard Odoms, Jr. He was the first person to put forth the idea that I write a book about my experience working in the Philadelphia Prison System and improving the lives of my students. His encouragement has meant a great deal to me in both professional and personal terms. For that, I am very grateful.

I am grateful to my wife and daughter, Eileen and Toni, for their support. They have endured my stress, procrastination, and excitement as I worked through many drafts of this book.

I want to thank and recognize my valued colleague, Carolyn E. Paige, longtime assistant principal and administrative assistant at Pennypack House School, for her close readings and edits of the manuscript and her contribution to chapter 9. She has worked professionally with me since 2001 and continues to be a trusted advisor and close friend. Her support and coordination of the academic programs and her commitment to help even the hardest-struggling students is praiseworthy.

The understanding and experience that enabled me to write this book was fostered by many professional and highly valued colleagues and friends, over many years. Wylie J. Hinson, Bryant Horsley, Frank Garritano, and Ronald J. Cage have contributed to my professional development and success. I appreciate the mentorship of these remarkable educators and individuals, and I am very grateful for the opportunity to have had my professional career shaped, guided, and influenced by them.

Hilderbrand Pelzer, Jr., and Gloria Pelzer, my parents, and my brother Tyrone Pelzer, are also remarkable educators and individuals. Their guidance and ongoing support continues to encourage my endeavors in the field of education.

Finally, my appreciation and thanks especially goes to the wonderful students and teachers with whom I've worked and the entire Philadelphia Prison System community. All helped me execute an extraordinary educational experience at Pennypack House School.

Introduction

PEOPLE WHO ARE frustrated with public schools often make strong statements: "Their failure to educate our children is a crime." "Schools are in crisis." "Our children are attending schools that look like prisons." "Schools are dangerous places." "The conditions in schools are deplorable." "Teachers are drowning in society's ills." "Our children are in trouble." "Get violent children out of the schools."

No doubt, these comments are fueled by negative experiences and the unsettling headlines and images of public schools that are plastered across the media; but, they do nothing to change the situation. Through my experiences, I've learned that negative comments about public schools actually help to handcuff the great potential that lies within them. I once led a public school that looked and felt like a prison. It was a place where failure abounded, danger lurked, and learning was threatened. The students were some of the city's most violent and hardest to reach. Despite those daunting challenges, my staff and I were able to "unlock" the potential of the school in ways that allowed students to thrive and experience academic learning.

In his book *Raggedy Schools: The Untold Truth*, educator Dr. Steve Perry states, "Urban principals, more than any others, must see where we want our schools to be and commit our blood to getting there." I cannot agree more with Dr. Perry. Principals and other school and school district educators hold the power to make education come alive for young people. Too often adults, most critically parents and educators, give up on children—they simply stop believing in them. "I'm tired of talking to you." "Talking to you is like talking to a brick wall." "I give up." "You'll never learn." "You will find yourself either dead or in jail if you don't change your ways." "I don't care what you do anymore." These statements signal that adults have lost patience—they believe they have done everything conceivable to bring change and order to their children's lives, to no avail. To children, hearing these statements bring extreme frustration.

Since my earliest days as a teacher, I've found myself drawn to the challenge of working with struggling and reluctant learners and with schools that have thrown up their hands in frustration. This book draws on my professional experiences and my work in public education within the Philadelphia Prison

System. My purposes in writing it are to examine public education from an angle that is under-represented in national debates and to present my own approach, based on a successful program for educating incarcerated school-age youths in the Philadelphia Prison System, to confronting the legal, logistical, and educational dilemmas that have thwarted such programs. Outlined in this book are strategies that educators and corrections professionals, working with incarcerated youths, can use to review their educational practices; examine their assumptions about the capacities and capabilities of schools in prisons; plan action to overcome legal, logistical, and educational dilemmas; and raise educational dialogue to the level that such work merits. I believe these strategies will be especially helpful to people working with school-age youth in local or county adult detention centers and correctional facilities.

Across the country, local governments that operate adult detention centers and correctional facilities, along with their school-district partners, are facing some difficult times and tough decisions about reaching and teaching a population of school-age youths that much of the public doesn't know exist. Sometimes, a school has to fight a negative tide. On my arrival at Pennypack House School as its principal, I was faced with a long-standing legal complaint against the prison system and the School District of Philadelphia for denying direct-file/certified juveniles an education. I had to act right away, even though I was awed by the task. To achieve the program coherence and capacity solutions that were needed, I had no choice but to reform the public education services available to the school district's incarcerated school-age youths. I also had to address and resolve the legal, logistical, and educational dilemmas affecting school operation and students' academic performance

With my work in the prison system off to a quick start, I knew I was facing an opportunity to make extraordinary changes. I, also, knew that under prison system circumstances the changes would have to be quick, flexible, reliable, and affordable.

CHAPTER 1

The Ills of Public Schools

THROUGHOUT THE UNITED States, especially in large cities and poor neighborhoods, public schools are failing to reach, teach, and engage thousands of struggling youths who are defeated by the schools they attend, whether because of poor educational backgrounds, reluctance to be in the school environment, or both. As a result of these failures, thousands of school-age youths are represented among the rising inmate population in correctional facilities. They struggled greatly before setting off on the path from public school student to dropout, and then to crime perpetrator and prison inmate.

You have surely seen the news stories that color many people's perceptions about public schools: Students cannot read, write, or perform math at grade level. High schools struggle as graduation rates slump. Nearly one in three U.S. high school students do not receive a graduation diploma. Serious violence occurs often in urban schools, and students everywhere suffer from bullies. Numbers of school-age youth are on a self-imposed journey to prison. How can a school let such things happen? According to today's typical news story, it is the principal's fault that the school does not perform and students do not achieve.

Here is an example of what schools and their principals face. According to subsequent trial testimony, five Philadelphia high school students left their school about lunchtime on March 26, 2008, and headed for a downtown mall. Later that day, they met a friend who dared them to beat up the first person they saw in the subway. Sean Patrick Conroy, the manager at a downtown Starbucks, was that person. One of the students rushed up behind Sean Conroy and began punching him in the head. The others followed. By the time the Philadelphia police arrived on the scene, Sean Conroy's lungs were so overinflated from an acute asthma attack that he could not speak. He died in a nearby hospital emergency room. "The high school students had chosen their victim at random and attacked him for no reason other than to amuse themselves," police said. "He just happened to be walking in front of them and they picked him out," said a homicide detective investigating the case. The students were arraigned on murder and conspiracy charges because the victim had had a severe asthma attack and died. The Philadelphia district attorney's office tried and convicted them as adults.

Of all the violent crimes that have taken place in Philadelphia in recent years, this one most acutely brings home to me the senseless journey to prison that many youths seem to be eagerly pursuing. Police noted that the fatal attack had occurred at 2:35 p.m. on a weekday. The five students should have been in school; instead, they had sought out an innocent man and attacked him violently—for amusement. The first youth to be apprehended had never been involved in criminal activities and had no prior police record. What a pathetic decision! It cost him and the others their freedom and their families' shame. It cost the Conroy family an immeasurable, long-lasting heartache.

The crime committed against Sean Conroy was not the principal's fault. It was not the school's fault, nor the school district's. It was not the parents' fault. It was the youths' fault. At ages fifteen through seventeen, they made a decision that changed their lives forever. By all accounts, the students' intent was to assault and perhaps commit a robbery, but not to commit a murder; they were spared a life sentence. However, they will spend the next thirteen to twenty-five years of their lives in prison. I'm sure the lessons they are learning now are much less exciting and inspiring than the lessons that were waiting for them at school that fateful day.

It appears that many school-age youths are learning some extremely difficult lessons as a result of their reckless decisions and criminal behavior. Without question, we can spread some of the blame for students' difficulties and lack of interest in school on multiple factors. Inadequate classroom education, poor academic skills, and little supervision are a few ingredients fueling the problems of serious misbehavior. However, students themselves must accept some blame for choosing to pursue crime over acquiring an education.

Attaining an education is the single most important resource that enables a person to prosper in society, create and take advantage of life's opportunities, and develop and strengthen the skills and strategies necessary to sustain a high-performing life. Society has a responsibility to guide youth toward educational attainment and to assist them in avoiding pitfalls that could cause their destruction. If we don't accept this challenge, many youths are left with far too little education to sustain them. Shut out of the mainstream and lacking the education to compete for employment or college opportunities, they seek thrills in criminal behavior, bolstered by immaturity, friendships of others like themselves, and heartbreaking, dead-end decisions.

My grandmother, Jessie Mae Pelzer, once said, "If you don't have an education, you won't get a job. If you don't have a job, you won't have any money. If you don't have any money, you will steal." Enough said! My grandmother's logic was basic; but, it made a strong case for education. The last time I checked, public education was still free, anywhere in the United States. Yet, millions of school-age youths decide to skip school on a regular basis or simply drop out. Nothing good can possibly come from skipping school or dropping out. Ask the five youths who attacked Sean Conroy and unwittingly committed murder.

In the early twentieth-century, the promise of public schools was to foster young people's development and ensure their academic and occupational preparation. This promise has been broken. Today, it is almost obsolete, based on the large numbers of high school dropouts and undereducated youth facing doubtful futures. Many students are performing below basic levels in most major subject areas, both on state tests and in classroom performance, especially in reading, writing, and math. These core subjects represent the foundations of education. Without competency in these basic subject areas, there is little hope for our youth.

One major reason for the downward spiral of public schools is that the original promise has not kept pace with societal changes. Schools now deal with multiple waves of technological advances, a fast-changing youth culture, changing architecture and school building requirements, neighborhood revitalization efforts, and changing demographics. These changes affect the relationships of schools and their neighborhoods, for both better and worse. The performance of public schools affects the overall health and future vitality of neighborhoods. For example, the level of academic accomplishment affects the property values of entire neighborhoods and cities. Unfortunately, entire neighborhoods and cities are deteriorating. They are becoming crime-ridden as a result of students' poor academic performance, the failures of public schools, and a lack of employment opportunities.

Low teacher quality and teachers' lack of bravery in undertaking the teaching of struggling or highly reluctant learners plays a major role in creating educational gaps between student groups. Teachers' low expectations often undermine the educational and academic progress of the very students they are responsible for educating. Components of teacher quality include planning meaningful lessons, delivering instruction, working to encourage improvements in individual student performance, and monitoring academic progress. Teacher commitment—the will to educate all students, regardless of ethnicity, social status, parental support, and poverty—must emanate from within each individual teacher. The key is the desire to deliver instruction to other people's children with the same veracity, intensity, and desire for success that one would offer one's own children.

In researching her book *Through Their Eyes, a Strategic Response to the National Achievement Gap*, educational consultant Dr. Kay lovelace found that high school students felt that much of their high school work was the same as what they had done in elementary school and that it allowed them little opportunity to prepare for the future. Many veteran teachers and staff, with their decades-old teaching styles and blind support of the status quo, actually hold back students who live in our technological age. These teachers fail to become knowledgeable about new instructional strategies and remain unaware of developing research in public education, youth culture, and strategies for meeting the academic needs of students who may be hard to reach.

The media also shares the blame for the failing outcomes of public schools. The public education debate within state legislatures, boards of education, and elsewhere often consists of half-truths ripped from the headlines—geared not toward promoting successful academic outcomes but to sensationalizing the negative. Media outlets seem to believe they will gain economic mileage by plastering negative stories and images on the pages of newspapers and seeking out stories that focus on the social ills, poverty, and the failures of schools. Television images reinforce the idea that huge numbers of young people are dangerous and ineducable. When young people are involved in violence or crime during non-school hours or during the summer months when school is not in session, it is *youth* violence; but when the same actions occur in or around schools during the school year, it is *school* violence.

Many times, the media focuses in on youth crimes in minority or poor neighborhoods, thereby obscuring and denying the efforts of the many families who are raising good, wholesome young people in the same areas. When a crime in or around a neighborhood school occurs during the school year, the entire school community is smeared. The media, joining hands with meddlesome and divisive politicians, business professionals, individuals, and organizations, often overlooks opportunities to help public schools promote academic success. Neither the media nor these politicians and organizations have been heard to advocate that public schools couple their core academic missions with programs and services that aim to eradicate the social ills and poverty surrounding public education. It is as though these officials intended to build their political power and organizational territory on the backs of students—their real aim often seems to be to coerce school districts into using their resources to assist them in bringing forward their political agendas.

Politicians, business professionals, individuals, and organizations frequently place burdens on public schools by pressuring them to execute convoluted, competing, and often redundant initiatives for remedial education and for programs in preventing violence, drug abuse, teenage pregnancy, and gangs. Overlapping programs compete for funding from the same sources and for attention from the same school organizations: gender and sexuality education and awareness, STD testing in schools, antipoverty initiatives, job development, at-risk youth, and multiple other social services. One could make a compelling case that these external "partners" thrive on the digressions of failing students and public schools. Most of these initiatives do have some merit and educational value. However, should they displace the academic mission of our schools at a time when educators need to focus on students' academic development?

An informal survey conducted, by me, of a random sample of Philadelphia urban school principals shows that urban public schools are likely to have the following characteristics:

- Below-average test scores on standardized examinations
- Crumbling school buildings and out-of-date classrooms and equipment
- Significant numbers of students returning from incarceration with few academic credits, or none at all
- Large numbers of students who require special education services
- Large numbers of over-age students who lack credits toward graduation
- Instructional fragmentation
- Meager or substandard funding

Survey data, face-to-face conversations, and field observations have provided ample support for my claim that the academic mission is being compromised. It should not be.

What is not mentioned in the list above is the erosion of trust between students and the schools that results from these conditions. Public schools sometimes rely on police responses and student arrests as methods of disciplinary control. Teachers dole out poor grades as a method of discipline. These factors widen the distrust between students and their schools. Trust should be supported, not dismantled.

Public schools should establish relationships and collaborations with various public and private partners who are working to have positive, significant impact on student development and teaching and learning. The instructional core in public schools should not be subjected to political whim or educational fashion. Instead, the core should be imploded, with the aim of destroying outdated practices and rebuilding public education. The rebuilding process should include innovations to address all aspects of the school community that contribute to student achievement.

Out of the wreckage, schools should develop a public education model that advances a new vision for invigorating teaching and learning and student achievement. School districts and their public schools must acquire teaching talent and foster an environment and culture in which the entire school community feels free to pursue ideas. Although there is plenty of blame to share for the condition of the schools and the hindrances to academic progress, I say emphatically that students should not be let off the hook. Apathy toward attaining academic knowledge and pursuing educational opportunities is senseless. Some students willfully engage in reckless and criminal behaviors and devalue the educational process—these actions and attitudes contribute to ruining their lives. These students haven't figured out that the "cost" of completing an education is less expensive than the cost of stupidity.

The high-school graduate population of the United States was once a large, productive percentage of the workforce; but, the population has been shrinking fast for almost two decades due to school-age youths failing to complete high school. Today, dropouts between the ages of sixteen and twenty-four are finding themselves unemployed. Those who are employed usually labor in meaningless, temporary, and dead-end jobs. Additionally, with the college admissions process getting more competitive, the shrinking base of high school graduates is forcing colleges and universities to revamp recruitment efforts to sustain the same level and quality of students as once enrolled.

In a speech to the National Press Club, then U.S. Secretary of Education Rod Paige said, "Those who are unprepared will sit on the sidelines; confronting poverty, dead-end jobs, and hopelessness . . . They will find little choice and much despair. The well-educated will live in a world of their own choosing; the poorly educated will wander in the shadows." This statement reminded me of my grandmother's statement about education, jobs, and crime. These harsh words, coming from the nation's top education official, are a loud alarm, waking us up to the necessity that it is time for public school students to take charge of their destiny. They will need to amass strategies, knowledge, and skills for improvement.

A study by the Bill and Melinda Gates Foundation found that students in a handful of big-city school districts have less than a fifty-fifty chance of graduating from high school with their peers. The study showed that fourteen urban school districts have graduation rates lower than 50 percent; these include: Detroit, Baltimore, New York City, Milwaukee, Cleveland, Los Angeles, Miami, Dallas, Denver, Houston, and Washington, D.C. Of the fourteen, three districts graduate less than forty percent. Low graduation rates are found throughout the United States and present a crisis of epic proportions for the future. Former U.S. Secretary of State Colin Powell has said, "When more than 1 million students a year drop out of high school, it's more than a problem, it's a catastrophe."

While the term "dropout" is usually associated with high schools, there is evidence that students are now dropping out of middle and elementary schools. It is not unusual for inmates in the Philadelphia Prison System to describe their middle school years as the time they began the journey from public school student to dropout and then from crime to prison. Anthony, convicted at age fifteen, is serving five to ten years at the Pine Grove State Correctional Institution, a prison in Western Pennsylvania for juveniles convicted of adult crimes. In an interview with *The Philadelphia Inquirer*, he offered his insights on middle school: "It was a bad experience. Nobody was going to class. People were bringing guns to school and having sex inside the bathrooms. It wasn't even a school." Jamil, arrested for murder at fifteen and sentenced to life in prison, echoed Anthony's remarks. Jamil recalls that he was a good student, "Then in middle school, I started messing up."

The longer academic deficiencies and other educational difficulties persist, the less likely it is that remediation will be successful. Research suggests students who do not read by the fourth grade have only a 12 percent probability of ever learning to read.

Incarcerated school-age youths are among the growing student population in correctional facilities. Large numbers of them are marginally literate or illiterate and have dropped out or been pushed out of public school or have experienced repeated failures. Most of these school-age youths are black males. In the Philadelphia Prison System, a history of school failure, low interest in school, and academic deficiency are commonplace.

Incarcerated youths differ substantially from their peers in educational attainment, lagging three or more years behind. I have found that on average they are below sixth-grade level in math and reading. Not having learned to read independently is the single most important weakness among incarcerated school-age youth; typical effects include not understanding or using a wide vocabulary, problems in using a dictionary and other reference materials, and a demonstrable difficulty with reading fluency and comprehension. However, basic mathematical computation requires the most instructional attention; data indicate that significant progress will be required to meet performance goals.

While education in prison is an under-recognized aspect of public education, rarely considered in the larger public education debate, it is growing in importance. According to the U.S. Bureau of Justice Statistics, more than 90 percent of state prisons provide some kind of education program for their inmates. Half of state prison inmates report that they have participated in an educational program since their most recent admission to prison. Yet, over half the inmates that I spoke with in the Philadelphia Prison System said the main reasons they had quit school were academic problems or a loss of interest in school.

The conditions of incarceration can help renew interest in school and in making educational progress.

Ultimately, however, school-age youths have to begin making better decisions about their public school situations and their futures. They don't need to wait and end up in prison to learn that they can graduate from high school.

CHAPTER **2**

Educational Despair—Up Close

DURING THE SUMMER of 1989, I got an up-close look at what life is like for people who lack the personal maturity, preparedness for life, and access to opportunities necessary for a good education. After graduating from Hampton University, I worked briefly for the Newport News (Virginia) Public Schools during the day and for the Newport News Department of Parks and Recreation in the evening; but, soon returned to Philadelphia to take a job as recreation director for a company that operated scattered site housing for homeless women and their children throughout the city. Scattered site housing is multifamily buildings, generally smaller than typical low income public housing properties, located in poor concentrated neighborhoods. Although I never intended this job to be a career move, the despair I saw in the homeless women and their children fueled my aspirations from that point on.

After just a few days at my new job, I was over-whelmed by the desperate situation of the women and their children. They were homeless, poor, unskilled, and uneducated. How did so many women with three, four, or even five children find themselves in such a predica-ment? What had happened in their lives to bring them to this despair? The women seemed to accept that the life they were living was the life meant for them. They had no plans to change their situations. My parents and fam-ily had given me all the support they could; I could not fathom the idea of falling into similar despair.

After just three months on the job, the compa-ny informed me that the city was not renewing its contract with them and my services were no lon-ger needed. I couldn't figure it out—how, in just three months, I could be employed and then unem-ployed? I figured out later what had really happened. Despite company executives boasting to me during my interviews about the high value they placed on recreational services for the homeless women and their children ("an important psychological diver-sion from the daily circumstances of their lives"; "strengthening family ties"), I soon saw that the com-pany's "commitment" to provide homeless women and their children with recreational services was only a strategy to hold on to its funding. Indeed, it was in the business of capitalizing on the booming economy surrounding the struggles of families and homelessness.

My experiences in this job fueled my desire to work in education. These experiences allowed me to observe people who did not have the abilities typically derived from education, to gain insight into their situations, and to consider ways to help them change. I felt this was very important; without help, they would forever be exploited.

About two weeks later, I saw a newspaper advertisement for a physical education teacher. The position required teaching experience and the ability to work with juvenile offenders incarcerated at the Bensalem Youth Development Center, a state juvenile correctional facility about twenty miles outside Philadelphia. What was not in the ad was the information that the Bensalem center housed most of the state's violent juvenile offenders. Armed with my degree in physical education and one year of teaching experience, I applied for the job. I had no work experience with juvenile offenders, nor did I have any experience in a correctional setting. But I needed a job! Also, I had a virtuous feeling about the challenges of the job and the good I would be able to do. I believed that I could make a difference in the lives of these young people. About a week after applying for the job, I was invited to interview for the position.

I expected a traditional interview, one-on-one with a human resources employee. Instead, a team of fifteen juvenile offenders conducted the interview. They interrogated me on parenthood, fatherhood, my relationships, my interests, my family, my childhood, and topics such as trust and commitment. Not once did anyone ask me about my ability to teach.

I got the job. Simple, let's get started, right? Not quite! From the first day, it was clear to me that four years of college had not prepared me for this teaching assignment. I was standing between education, on one side, and juvenile incarceration, on the other. Sink or swim. Five years later, I was swimming like a champion athlete. My students had been able to gauge my ability to be a successful teacher by carefully analyzing my responses to their interview questions. For my part, I worked very hard to become an effective, compassionate teacher. In retrospect, I am convinced that my ability to establish a genuine relationship with my students and help them to manage tough issues was an essential skill for improving student achievement.

I had a wonderful time teaching physical education and coaching the basketball team; but, my professional strengths were challenged by an experience that remains close to my heart up to this day. On days when the Bensalem center principal was away, the very capable assistant principal, Bryant Horsley, took over for him and I in turn took over Horsley's role as instructional supervisor. My job was to keep an eye on the teachers, student behaviors, instructional activities, and on the interaction between students and teachers. This assignment gave me considerable insight into what life is like for young people who do not have educational skills.

I saw the abysmal levels of illiteracy. I saw hundreds of juvenile offenders struggling with the learning process. Mostly black males, they were unable to read, write, or perform tasks at even a basic level. Many of them could not write in cursive or use calculators; their mathematics skills were far below marginal. Their attention span was not more than five minutes. Their grammar was nonexistent, and their spelling was a loss. The word "learn" became "lurn"; "teacher was spelled "teger." The word "principal" was "prenzabul," and "education was "edjaksion." Run-on sentences ran off the paper. Some students could not even spell their first or last names; some did not know their date of birth. They were pathetically uneducated, to the point of fear and aversion. As far as learning and developing learning skills, they seemed to want no part of it.

They were not alone. I often see students sleepwalking through school and life. They reject education as if it were a deadly disease. Some even proclaim they would rather fail or go to prison, or just live the street life, than pursue an education.

As Bensalem's physical education teacher, I saw young boys who were coarse, fearless, physically strong, and expressive; but, such was not the case when I assumed the instructional duties of the assistant principal. I saw just the opposite. For instance, I saw young boys who were mentally weak, apathetic toward learning, lifeless in the midst of lively classroom environments, and devastatingly fearful of school. Seeing those struggling and reluctant students day after day kept me perplexed. I began to doubt the school's mission—it seemed unattainable. How could we expect these juvenile offenders to meet the same challenging academic standards and attain the lasting achievements of their peers? They were so far behind the educatlonal curve that it seemed impossible for them to ever catch up. To reduce or eliminate the overwhelming academic deficiencies in many of our students, we would literally have to become miracle workers. A miracle worker I was not, or so I thought.

Despite my initial feeling that the school's mission was not attainable, I saw that Wylie J. Hinson, the dynamic and politically astute principal, was determined to lead the school and its students to success. Principal Hinson believed firmly in each juvenile offender's academic ability; in turn, the teachers believed in it too. Within a juvenile correctional institution, this principal created a school model that fostered successful student-teacher relationships. Even when an individual student did something very damaging, even ruinous, to the relationships that were being developed, the principal would model for his teachers the appropriate adult behavior to mend it.

My colleague Frank Garritano and I were very frequently on the receiving end of these modeled lessons. As the youngest teachers on the staff, Principal Hinson always placed us in situations that would test our commitment to our students. Those lessons definitely withstood the test of time. They are vivid in my mind and of great value to me today. Principal Hinson broadened professional development opportunities to help teachers learn to satisfy the learning needs of juvenile offenders. He made a concerted effort to ensure that each juvenile offender attended school daily and succeeded in the classroom. As I observed his efforts, it became clear to me that our school's mission was attainable. Even today, I believe strongly that rigorous instruction in classrooms, facilitated by strong instructional leaders, is the key ingredient in improving student achievement, within the correctional system and outside of it.

After several years at the Bensalem Youth Development Center, I began thinking seriously about how I could play a larger part in furthering the academic achievement of struggling and reluctant students and in improving the lives of people who do not have education-derived abilities. I had thought about this a lot when I worked with homeless mothers and their children. I was convinced that in sharing so much with me about their plights my incarcerated students were indirectly daring me to teach them and make things better for them and for others in similar situations. Many classroom interactions and many circumstances gave me a firsthand look at the power of education.

As I thought about my experiences and absorbed the lessons in leadership and commitment I had learned from Wylie Hinson, I made one of the biggest decisions of my life. I decided to replace my original career goal, sports management, with a new career goal: education administration. I wanted to be a principal. I wanted to be an educational leader who would be in charge of improving the academic performance of struggling and reluctant school-age students and challenge them to beat the risks facing their generation and restore hope for their futures. My strongest motivation was that I believed, then and now, that educational opportunity and academic achievement can uplift people and give them a chance to improve the quality of their lives.

My experience in the juvenile correctional environment had given me valuable insight into the disheartening results of educational disparities. Now I found myself challenged professionally to do something about what I had seen. I believe that education can turn around the situations of many urban families and youths and uplift entire neighborhoods.

CHAPTER 3

The White School Buses

AFTER LEAVING THE Bensalem Youth Development Center in 1994, I continued teaching, first at Chester High School in the Chester-Upland School District between Philadelphia and Wilmington and then at Roosevelt Middle School in the School District of Philadelphia. In 1997, I was appointed assistant principal at Simon Gratz High School, in the Nicetown-Tioga section of North Philadelphia, a worn industrial area.

Simon Gratz's principal, Ronald J. Cage, had dedicated himself to turning around this large, comprehensive high school, which served 2400 students in grades 9 through 12. Cage, a charismatic and intelligent leader with dynamic communication skills, had a handle on everything that was happening at the school. As principal, Cage focused on developing operational and instructional coherence. Under his leadership, the school broadened its focus on quality school programs. His instruction, to me, was to put structures and processes in place that would lead to a better school climate and to create an environment conducive for students to learn. In addition, I was responsible for all non-instructional operations. Little did I know that my previous experience with juvenile offenders would enable me to succeed in my role and to assist Principal Cage in achieving his vision for the school. My professional years under this principal's leadership were some of my finest. I was able to develop valuable administrative and leadership skills.

One day in the summer of 2000, Principal Cage gave me a shock when he told me he had decided to pursue another principalship opportunity. I couldn't believe it! He had expended tremendous amounts of energy to develop staff, students, and the entire school community. He also told me that he planned to recommend and support me for the principalship of Simon Gratz. With just three years of experience as an assistant principal, I was excited and scared at the same time. Then, he said something that struck me very deeply: "With all the work over the past three years on improving the school climate and the facility, next year has to focus on improving instruction." My feelings of excitement and apprehension immediately shifted to being just plain scared; and, my thoughts flashed back to the days at Bensalem Youth Development Center when I first decided to become a principal. The day of reckoning was here! I was going to get my chance to lead a school and improve the academic performance of students.

In September 2000, I became principal of Simon Gratz. During my tenure, I led a wonderful school community. With the help of my assistant principals and the school leadership team, we achieved many academic and educational successes, including implementing a national research-based school reform model that generated a sustained three-year gain in attendance, percentage of courses passed, and the persistence rate of ninth grade classes to graduation. The number of students attending college increased. Many students overcame challenges of poverty, homelessness, teenage parenthood, and community violence to achieve in academics, creative and performing arts, athletics, and student leadership. In September 2002, Prince Andrew, Duke of York, visited Simon Gratz to help launch the Jubilee International Education Fund, a program that sent some of our students to Great Britain for an expanded service learning curriculum and international studies. One year later, I left Simon Gratz High School.

In 2003, I was assigned by the School District of Philadelphia to lead the turnaround of another Philadelphia high school, Charles Carroll. Carroll, at that time, was an alternative school serving an average of 275 underperforming students who returned to school after dropping out of neighborhood high schools around the city. At the time, Charles Carroll was known for operating the longest-running student reclamation and reengagement program in Philadelphia and had achieved national recognition. However, its classrooms were sparsely populated, with no more than twelve students in each. Worse, the school was under mandate to right itself after failing to demonstrate academic progress for five consecutive years.

I saw right away that I needed to perform academic triage, and quickly. My first goal was to build the support systems needed to encourage students to return to school. Recruiting young people from across the city led to increased enrollment. An on-site child-care center was opened to support teenage parents, and other student support services were offered. A careful analysis of course alignments indicated that some students were enrolled in classes that would not help them fulfill the requirements for graduation; so, it was necessary to realign courses to support students' academic goals.

Students were offered an analysis of where they stood in terms of courses completed, help in selecting their classes, and course counseling so that they understood clearly the academic criteria they needed to meet for graduation. It was a sad, yet an undeniable fact that many of these over-age students were academically "lost"; they had never had anyone review with them their personal academic credit profiles and had no clear idea of the requirements for graduation. Within a year, teachers and students, working together, had achieved measurable objectives in reducing the factors impeding student achievement.

In 2004, I was asked by the School District of Philadelphia to take over as principal of Pennypack House School, which operates within the city of Philadelphia's six major correctional facilities. The previous principal had retired. This position offered me what I think was my most rewarding leadership experience—one that I believe I was destined to have. I arrived for my first day at the sprawling complex of the Philadelphia Prison System, enthusiastic and ready to lead a new school community. Curran-Fromhold Correctional Facility was opened in 1995 and is the largest of the six institutions in the Philadelphia Prison System. Curran-Fromhold replaced Holmesburg Prison, a nineteenth-century fortress (1896) that was one of the most notorious prisons in the United States, the home of Philadelphia's worst and infamous criminals. Curran-Fromhold was named for Patrick N. Curran and Robert F. Fromhold, once warden and deputy warden at Holmesburg; both were murdered in a riot there on May 31, 1973. Now, Curran-Fromhold was the place where I started each workday.

The school office was located within the correctional facility. Each day, I had a first-hand look at life in one of the nation's largest urban county jail systems. I observed thousands of adult inmates as they went about their days in prison. Adult inmates arose early to go to work: food service, maintenance, landscaping, industry, assisting in the chapel, tutoring, sanitation, barbering, and assisting in the law library, among other jobs. Inmates might also see a doctor or another medical professional. Some attended faith-based services. They attended drug and alcohol prevention programs and art classes, took vocational training in multiple fields, attended education programs, and prepared for high school equivalency examinations (GED). Some received social services or attended special events.

Inmates got haircuts at the prison barbershop, participated in recreational activities and sports, and mingled in the prison yard. They studied in the law library, visited with family members, and bought personal items, snacks, and toiletries from the commissary. From time to time, horrible violent incidents exploded. I was reminded suddenly and often that I was living in the inmates' world. My commitment to understanding the prison environment helped me to navigate the system.

Each morning at 8:15 a.m., like clockwork, I parked my car in my reserved parking space outside the prison. Before I got out of the car, I would perform a personal ritual. I'd look around me: the Interstate 95 expressway traffic rumbling overhead, the low-custody adult inmates doing landscaping work on the prison grounds in their bright orange jumpsuits, prison system employees heading toward their offices and other work locations. Visitors would be arriving, even this early and often with babies and small children, to visit loved ones. Lawyers arrived early too, with stacks of folders and briefs clutched under their arms, to visit with their inmate clients.

The inmates in the nearby housing units looked out through tiny windows and tapped loudly on the glass, trying desperately to get the attention of people walking past. They used written signs to communicate with the outside and sometimes requested perverse favors. The tapping reminded me of Morse code signals. These inmates expended a great amount of time and energy to get the attention of people walking past, seeming to believe that someone would stop and hold a conversation or grant their requests. To my dismay, some did!

Another part of my personal ritual was waiting for the white school buses to ride past. The buses were an astonishing sight for me; they presented a vivid illustration of the path taken by many inmates from public school, to dropout, to crime, to prison. While most people associate school buses with children, the color yellow, and traveling to and from school, I found a new association, one that I saw reflected in my new school.

The white school buses are operated by the city's Sheriff's Department and the Philadelphia Prison System. Each day, the white school buses transport hundreds of inmates between state correctional institutions, between jails of the prison system, and to and from the Criminal Justice Center in downtown Philadelphia. The sight of hundreds of inmates being transported in the white school buses provoked me to think: What went wrong in the lives of these inmates?

How much value did these inmates place on their education before incarceration? Had they become fascinated with the prison culture? I would wonder what our society would be like if these inmates were traveling to and from college instead of to and from a criminal court. And, I'd think further: Who is responsible for their plight? Family? School? Society? Is poverty itself an express ticket to prison?

Thinking ahead, I would ask myself what kinds of opportunities would be available to these inmates upon their reentry into society? What kinds of opportunities would be denied? Given the answers, what must a correctional education curriculum offer? What did the public education system do to serve these men and women? Was it adequate? What percentage of inmates came from well-heeled families able to offer educational and financial support? Does assignment to special education classes in a high school propel an individual to drop out, to commit a crime, and accept going to prison? Why aren't school districts actively engaged in the correctional education process? What percentage of inmates has undiagnosed mental health disorders? Why are black males incarcerated at a higher rate than non-black males? Why are so many black people, men and women, in prison? Why are so many black school-age youths charged as adults? What is the relationship between school failure and going to prison?

Could it be that some adults see prison as providing a stable quality of life that includes housing, health care, education, food, relationships, and employment? Are public education's failures playing a role in the increasingly complex and growing prison industry? What is going through the minds of the inmates as they travel to and from court? And then came the really hard question: What can I do to improve the quality, rigor, and role of public education in the lives of incarcerated school-age youths?

The white school buses and the prisoners that rode them served as a constant reminder of why I became a principal. All the questions I asked as I watched the white buses resurfaced as I was writing this book. How will others answer them?

CHAPTER 4

Why School?

"SCHOOL! KEY UP!" To alert correctional officers of my presence inside of House of Correction, I would shout "School! Key up!" whenever I was approaching one of the secured areas where male juvenile inmates entered or exited from one area of the prison to another. The shout meant that I or another member of the school staff was waiting to enter or exit the secured area.

Walking into the secured areas at the House of Correction was like walking into the nineteenth century. The facility's spoke-and-wheel design dates to correctional architecture of the early 1800s. Correctional officers holding huge black metal keys are stationed at each area portal and at the entrance to each cellblock to open and close prison cell bars and monitor inmate movement. They make sure that no one passes through except those authorized to do so. My visits to see "the boys," as I called them, required special alertness and attentiveness on the part of the officers. Juvenile inmates require a special level of security because they must have sight-and-sound separation from adult inmates to avoid risk of serious injury or other harm.

Among the thousands of individuals admitted to the Philadelphia Prison System annually and those detained or sentenced on any given day are between thirteen and seventeen years old, mostly males. Even after working within the prison system, I was always dismayed at the number of male school-age youths who entered the prison system each week. I am still not sure which is worse, the crimes (including murders) committed by those youths or the district attorney who brought the full weight of the office to bear in charging school-age youths as adults, trying them under the fullest extent of the law and working single-mindedly in court to send them to prison for most or all of their lives. Sometimes their trials would last only a day or two. This was troublesome in so many ways, and it demonstrated clearly how children were treated when their families had little to no resources to acquire a legal defense in court.

I often asked myself, "Do the young people who receive long sentences in an adult prison ever reflect on their incarceration and what caused it? Would they now be willing to take another look at education, and perhaps embrace it? Would their families be supportive of them during their long incarceration? How would they adjust to life in prison? Would they survive?"

At the same time, I wondered what would become of the young inmates. They seemed not to have any regard for the value of their lives or the lives of others. They were steadfast in their convictions that there was no harm or wrong in their actions. Their actions and choices were so interwoven with ignorance and lack of insight that they did not believe their own situations were serious or that their choices could be—or could have been—any different. Their attitude seemed to say, "That's just the way it is."

It was not unusual for me to hear young inmates talk openly and unapologetically about their crimes: "I got a body." "He's here for murder." "He came gunning after me, so I went after him." "That's the dude that shot the cop." "I can do whatever time they give me." "I shot him, so what?" More disheartening is the lack of understanding or caring that their criminal actions toward others had ultimately hurt themselves.

Many of the incarcerated youth showed a naïve or stubborn refusal to acknowledge reality and little or no understanding of the magnitude of their crimes or the consequences to follow. Many thought that their situation was far less serious than it actually was, even though they were behind bars. After all, they were able to receive frequent visits from family members and recognize familiar surroundings or city landmarks when being transported to and from court, for now. They were still in Philadelphia.

Some young men adapted quickly to incarceration; it was not until they were in the midst of their trials that they began to realize that their time in prison could very well go beyond incarceration in the local county jail. Indeed, their incarceration could and often did lead to unimaginable long years in state correctional institutions in parts of Pennsylvania they had never heard of.

It's very sad that so many youths *meant* to commit crimes they did but never considered the long-term, life-altering consequences. They were now inside the prison culture and would have to deal with forces capable of seducing and dominating a person. They would grow up in prison and stay there, seeing their world shaped by very close interactions with other imprisoned men.

To help young inmates resist seduction and domination, I believe it was paramount for my staff and me to ensure that our students were provided with structures that enabled effective use of their incarceration time. Anything around them could be evil. Young inmates needed access to hands-on resources and ready support at all times to allow them to grow and develop. I do not pity their plight or make light of their crimes; but, it was clear that my students required not only opportunities to grow and become stronger, but also ways to escape the anguishing levels of fear and stress. In many instances, these juvenile inmates had made conscious decisions to commit crimes and now they had to take full responsibility for their decisions and actions, even in the midst of calamity.

However, it is possible, even as a young person's life evolves within prison walls, to make a purposeful effort to find educational success. By good fortune, school-age youths in Pennsylvania are subject to compulsory school attendance up to age seventeen. Thus, local school districts are responsible for providing educational services to school-age youths in local correctional facilities that fall within those districts. In the fall of 2004, I delivered an orientation talk to some newly enrolled young men. Pleased with my delivery and the points that I had made, I asked enthusiastically, "Does anyone have any questions?" A young man raised his hand politely. I was ready to clarify what I had just said about the school's mission and academic program; but, instead, the new enrollee blurted out, "Why do we have to come to school if we are in jail?" His question was asked in a very straightforward way, and he slid down onto the edge of his seat to hear my reply.

My answer was a typical response: "You must take advantage of educational opportunities, grow mentally, substantively, and meaningfully, even in jail." The students looked at me as if I hadn't even answered the question, or as if my answer was totally meaningless. I eventually learned that the question I'd been asked is very often on the mind of juvenile inmates, and it is one major reason that I was inspired to write this book. As I learned my way around the prison system, interacting with staff and inmates alike, I came to realize that my answer was the right one.

Consider Marquette, sixteen years old at the time, whom I first met in July 2006. Marquette was deferential in manner, and at our first meeting he courageously told me that he wanted to enroll in school because he could not read. From the time of that meeting until the day he was sentenced and transferred to a state prison, Marquette went from very low reading and writing proficiency to reading successfully and writing artistic poems about his life and aspirations. He found that he could excel in mathematics; his comprehension of algebra impressed everyone, especially those who knew he had arrived at the prison with very poor academic ability.

Marquette was typical of many of my students in that he came from poor educational circumstances. Where he differed was in his courageous zeal to learn. At each opportunity that we had to talk with each other, I was struck anew by his ambition to make up for the lost learning opportunities he had endured. When we talked about education, life, or Marquette's own experiences, he demonstrated determination and confidence to overcome the barriers in his life. I believe Marquette's strong desire to learn and become a successful student helped him come to grips with his crime. Over time, he was able to gain some insight into his prison circumstances and the events and decisions that had brought him there! And, he took full responsibility for his criminal action. He was able to file a plea that may permit his release from prison by the time he is 21.

Despite facing murder charges, 17-year-old Jerline proved, in prison, to be an outstanding, conscientious student. He was the living representation of Winston Churchill's famous statement, "I am always willing to learn, however I do not always like to be taught." During his trial, Jerline began to pull away from the relationship he had developed with the school and his teachers. All the adults and students around him noticed changes in his attitude, behavior, and school performance; but, no one attempted any direct intervention. His favorite teacher came to me with the information that Jerline was acting in unusual ways, misbehaving, disrupting classes, and refusing to do his school assignments. When I asked the teacher if he or anyone else had spoken with Jerline to ascertain the cause of his difficulties, he replied that no one had.

I sat down with Jerline to learn what was troubling him. What was causing him to pull away from the success he had been achieving in school? Jerline said abruptly, "I don't care anymore." I asked him what it was he didn't care about. He turned to me and shouted, "I don't care about school; it can't help me anymore."

Unbeknown to me, Jerline had recently been informed by his lawyer that he was facing twenty to forty years in prison for his crime. I listened to Jerline speak, erratically, about the impact that twenty to forty years behind bars would have on his life, I realized that his irrational behavior was coming from his struggle to make sense of his destiny. Jerline was, for perhaps the first time in his life, finding that he cared deeply about all the things that would have been part of his life if it were not for his poor decision to commit a violent crime. He talked about family, fatherhood, marriage, working for a living, homeownership, and growing old. For Jerline, at that moment, his entire future was out of reach and unattainable.

Our conversation continued over the next several days. It was very important, to me, that Jerline have the opportunity to talk through and gain insight into his circumstances and come to some understanding of living and growing up in prison. In instances like this, many juvenile inmates attempt to jump mentally to the end of the prison sentence, as if it were just around the corner. In actuality, their path to the end of a prison sentence is usually a decades-long journey.

Jerline used these conversations to face up to the errors he had made and to try to grasp the fact that he would serve up to forty years of his life in prison. He knew he could not escape the punishment waiting for him. I tried my best to encourage him to continue his education as he grew to adulthood in prison. He embraced my message to continue his schooling, learn to be resourceful, and try to avoid the many pitfalls of prison life. Eventually, Jerline received a sentence of seventeen to thirty-four years. His final words to me, before being transferred from the Philadelphia Prison System to a state correctional institution, were, "Thank you, I will be fine."

Marquette and Jerline are examples of what can happen for school-age youth in trouble when someone works to educate, motivate, and be patient with them. Like them, many others have the innate ability to learn and achieve at high levels. Consider yet another student, a 19-year-old inmate. As I sat in my office at Curran-Fromhold Correctional Facility one afternoon, a social worker stopped by my office and stepped into the doorway. She said, "Mr. Pelzer, thank you for testing my client for the GED certificate." I replied, "You're welcome," but I wasn't sure who her client was. Most of the GED tests were administered by my staff, not by me directly. Something, though, touched me about this enthusiastic expression of thanks.

The next day, I made it a point to meet with the GED examiners to inquire about the social worker's client. They informed me that he was "a special case" and explained that he had had to take the test under protective custody to protect him from other inmates, to protect other inmates from him, and to protect him from himself. They also mentioned that he had been very eager to earn a GED.

I was floored. Administering a GED test to an inmate within the boundaries of such restrictive security requires elaborate precautions, planning, and scheduling. I was curious about why the social worker had been so pleased and enthusiastic, and I prodded the examiners for additional information about the inmate. What was his age? What was so special about him and his situation? Was his criminal case currently in the news? Was he about to be transferred to a state correctional institution?

I learned, to my great surprise, that the social worker's client had recently been sentenced to death. He was just nineteen years old, and according to the examiners, he had requested an opportunity to take the GED test as a way to achieve something in his life and to give his family some way to be proud of him. He was about to be transferred to a state correctional institution for death-row inmates, ultimately to die. At that moment, it was clear to me that his request to earn a GED, in the face of a death sentence, was an incredible affirmation of the importance of education. It is instinctive in all of us, no matter what our situations in life, to do something to improve our lives or to do something well. What clearer demonstration could there be that education can improve and transform peoples' lives?

Consider yet another student, this time an older man. As I walked through the medical service area at the Philadelphia Industrial Correctional Center, a frantic adult inmate came out of nowhere to approach me. He wanted my immediate assistance to enroll in

GED preparation classes. Thinking that he might be having a problem getting a referral and needed my intervention just to smooth the enrollment process, I began to go through the steps he would have to take to enroll. In the middle of my explanation, he cut me off, "No, Principal Pelzer, I'm not having that kind of trouble, but I'm still in the damn Hooked on Phonics class and I want to get my GED!" I learned later that he was fifty-five years old.

While I could understand and feel the inmate's frustration, I had to think hard about what I should say. What type of response was he expecting? I did not want to say the wrong thing and have all hell break loose. The reality is that there were no words that I could provide but the truth. His frustration was not with me, nor the Hooked on Phonics class. What was frustrating him was carrying the burden of a lifetime of illiteracy. Just by chance, our paths had crossed. It was surreal. At that moment, on that day, in a prison, it was just the two of us, face to face. This inmate with his outburst had chosen to open the door of an educational opportunity that had been foreclosed when he was of school age. I explained to him that he had a steep hill to climb; and, I then saw that he got help making an individual academic plan. He soon began classes leading to a GED.

Kareem, a male juvenile inmate, told me bluntly, "I want to quit school." My response was nonchalant, since this request was typical among the juvenile inmates: "Why is that?" Kareem replied, "Because I'm 16 years old and still reading on first-grade level." I was at a loss for words, and my nonchalance quickly turned to concern. Here in front of me was a 16-year-old who was clearly aware of his educational deficiency and had the courage to present his problem directly to the school principal.

I found that Kareem was reading at a 1.2 reading grade level and performing at a 2.0 grade level in math. It was not uncommon to meet school-age youths with similar educational limitations. But for some reason, the helpless, yet firm tone of Kareem's voice compelled me to give him a reply that would breathe life back into his belief in school and assure him that his educational circumstance could be improved. Before I replied, I glanced over at my administrative assistant, trying to order my thoughts. My assistant, sensing my quandary, looked directly at Kareem, "I will help you if you want. I will tutor you weekly." Then, to me, she added, "Tutoring will help him build his literacy skills and self-confidence level."

My assistant treated Kareem as her son. Never did she discuss in his presence the discouraging fact that his reading and math skills were so low. She just worked with him. Kareem received individual tutoring until he was transferred to another correctional facility in another state. The individual tutoring had helped Kareem to feel good about himself, and he worked diligently with my assistant to improve his skills. After he was transferred, he wrote my assistant a letter. The letter was very elementary, but my assistant was deeply pleased that Kareem had gained enough confidence in himself to write to her.

Illiteracy in prison is an epidemic, as is the drop-out rate in public education. For many inmates, even younger ones, the experience of attending school is a distant memory. More important, the experience of success in school is nonexistent.

CHAPTER **5**

Headed Straight to Criminal Court

IF STATEMENTS ABOUT educating all children reflect a public education priority and not a cliché, we should be more than willing to educate students in prison, right?

Once school-age youths are incarcerated, what is society's obligation to ensure that they mature, become better human beings, and continue their education? Asking this question in no way suggests that we should pity children who commit serious and violent crimes and find themselves in prison. We shouldn't—and I don't. They deserve to be punished for criminal behavior. But, believe it or not, prison can be a very successful learning environment for people who cannot be reached through traditional teaching methods and haven't achieved success in school.

Politicians across the nation, responding to the public's call to get tough on crime, have demanded that school-age youths take responsibility for their crimes by being punished as adults. The number of young people incarcerated as adults is growing. Once detained or convicted by the adult criminal court system, these youths will have to find ways and exert effort to achieve success in life, inside or outside a prison.

The Rest of their Lives, a joint report by Amnesty International and Human Rights Watch, reveals that in forty-two states, as well as in federal jurisdictions, a person under eighteen who is suspected of a serious, violent crime can be tried as an adult for criminal justice purposes. There are many examples. In Camden, New Jersey, Zorn Torres, a 15-year-old boy, was tried as an adult on murder charges in the shooting of another teen. In Chester, Pennsylvania, 16-year-old Jammer Evans was held without bail after being charged as an adult with first-degree murder. Also in Chester, Michael Starlings was charged as an adult for attempted homicide and simple and aggravated homicide. In Fort Lauderdale, Florida, Michael Livingston, 16, and Patrick Keels, 17, were charged as adults with attempted second-degree murder. In Philadelphia, three teenagers were ordered to stand trial as adults on third-degree murder charges in the death of a pizza deliveryman who had a heart attack as he was being robbed while delivering a pizza they had ordered. Also in Philadelphia, two teenagers, 14 and 17 years old, were charged as adults with killing an 87-year-old Navy veteran during an attempted robbery because he "did not move fast enough."

These national headlines merely indicate the growing number of youths—many just children—who are tried and sentenced as adults. In November 1995, Pennsylvania, as 40 other states before it had done, enacted legislation (known as Act 33) that ordered automatic transfer to the adult courts of any juvenile charged with rape, nonconsensual deviant sexual intercourse, aggravated assault, armed robbery, theft of a motor vehicle, aggravated indecent assault, kidnapping, voluntary manslaughter, or an attempt, conspiracy or solicitation to commit murder. Act 33 has increased the population of school-age youths in local and county-operated adult detention centers and correctional facilities. Youths sentenced as adults are identified as direct-file/certified juveniles because they have bypassed filings and proceedings in family or juvenile courts and gone straight to criminal courts. If convicted in a criminal court, they are sentenced and transferred to a Pennsylvania Department of Corrections adult prison, often for decades. Strict-sentencing rules in Pennsylvania and automatic provisions in the law combine to put numbers of school-age youths behind bars for life. According to published reports, Pennsylvania has more school-age youths serving life in prison than any other jurisdiction in the world.

The national phenomenon of incarcerating school-age youths in adult correctional facilities is having dramatic effects on their education in jails and prisons. Balancing security demands with student achievement goals becomes ever more difficult and does not seem to be a priority in the national education debate. As school-age youths await trial in local or county-operated adult detention centers and correctional facilities, their mere presence creates tremendous legal, logistical, and educational dilemmas. For instance, adult inmate movement is often compromised to achieve the required separation (out of sight and sound) of youths and adults. Competing demands for the use of space, services, and programs require frequent negotiations, creative scheduling, and careful allocation of existing resources. At the same time, local school districts are mandated to operate public schools in correctional environments—schools that will offer juvenile inmates the same quality of education they would receive on the outside. The schools must also demonstrate that they are helping students progress to a high school diploma and postsecondary opportunities.

The trend of locking up juveniles in adult prisons does not appear to be declining. The practice of sentencing youths from two years to life in adult prisons is forcing state and federal adult correctional institutions to reprioritize their short and long-term educational planning and to implement new solutions for educating incarcerated school-age youths. A major factor hindering schools from providing educational opportunities for school-age youths is the type of security level and physical layout of correctional facilities. Findings from a national survey conducted by the Center for Effective Collaboration and Practice, a research organization focused on juvenile justice, showed that only 29 percent of juveniles in adult corrections facilities across the United States were enrolled in education programs. This fact is especially disturbing, because states have been transferring more and more youths from juvenile to criminal courts and from juvenile to adult correctional facilities. The study affirms that the type of correctional facility affects the availability of education to juveniles.

The Philadelphia Prison System made it a priority for all school-age youths, including those assigned to segregated areas and special management units, to participate daily in public education. Even students who were held under extreme security precautions and required handcuffs and leg shackles could leave their cells to go to a designated learning space with teachers, academic assistance, and access to the same core curriculum as their peers. Planning to meet logistical challenges and making education available to all juvenile inmates regardless of their classification was a major strategy for success.

While girls were incarcerated in the Philadelphia Prison System at a much lower rate than boys—until recently, girls represented just 15 percent of all school-age youths in custody—the proportion of girls in custody has been rising and mirrors national trends. The presence and lower proportion of female school-age youths holds some unique implications for educational equity. However, it is very important to the educational success of the girls that they receive the same opportunities and access as the boys.

Philadelphia's Riverside Correctional Facility for Women is a twenty-first century maximum-security facility for approximately 800 female adult inmates. The warden was very understanding of the educational equity implications for girls. Fewer girls were held in the adult women's prison than boys in the adult men's prison, and the proportion of girls to adult women prisoners was much smaller than the juvenile-adult ratio in the male prisons. The warden and his staff worked with me to ensure an educational environment that was conducive to learning and managed the legal, logistical, and educational challenges to ensure that the girls could flourish in the correctional setting.

Male school-age youths, however, were housed until September 2007 at the House of Correction, one of the oldest jails located on the correctional complex. It was the conditions in this prison that provoked a long-standing legal complaint against the Philadelphia Prison System and School District of Philadelphia. Extraordinary resourcefulness and flexibility were required to meet the challenge. The House of Correction, an antiquated stone fortress built in 1925 in the then-common spoke-and-wheel design, did not permit separation of adult and youth prisoners. It had 550 cells in six two-story stone wings radiating from a central rotunda, with no perimeter walls or observation towers. Social service offices, classrooms, and visiting areas were arranged around a newer entrance corridor leading to the rotunda. For decades, the Philadelphia Prison System's male school-age youths were held on just two cellblocks.

In September 2007, the male school-age youths were moved to a newer, larger facility on the correctional complex, the Philadelphia Industrial Correctional Center. Before the move, the prison system's deputy commissioner of operations asked me to conduct a walkthrough of the Philadelphia Industrial Correctional Center and provide my professional opinion about its suitability as a facility for the school-age youths. I was honored that my professional opinion mattered to the prison system officials, and it showed me that they were considering the educational outcomes for the youths who would be housed there. The Philadelphia Industrial Correctional Center, with its special management unit style of operation, spaciousness, and division between medium and maximum-security units, would clearly improve the management of the male school-age youths. Also, the special management unit would help decentralize the facility into smaller, more manageable units.

While correctional facility design should support the security demands required for housing incarcerated school-age youths, it should also support and contribute to realizing educational expectations. The Philadelphia Industrial Correctional Center had been designed to implement both unit management and vocational training. The Federal Bureau of Prisons had developed the basic component—the housing unit—and the operational procedures to support it in the early 1970s. While the Philadelphia Industrial Correctional Center does present its own legal, logistical, and educational services challenges, its design aspects, from its physical layout and environment to the emphasis on special management units, offered greater flexibility than the House of Correction. The design includes separate recreational yards, social service and medical triage areas and easy access for male school-age youths to classrooms and workshops.

Other factors affect the planning and implementation of quality educational programs for school-age youths in adult jails and prisons. Teachers struggle with juvenile inmates who have academic deficiencies and a wide range of learning gaps in basic education. Histories of educational failures abound, creating a high level of apathy. Furthermore, the correctional environment is cyclical, with inmates constantly brought in, discharged, and transferred. Cyclical enrollment and other factors contributing to rapid turnover have a tremendous effect on teacher planning, the classroom climate, and the instructional flow.

Cultivating buy-in and commitment to teaching and learning among the prison community's stakeholders is a constant challenge. Every day, schools in prisons, like the Pennypack House School, must collaborate with prison officials to comply with security requirements and prison management demands that cannot otherwise be accommodated. For instance, there are restrictions on specific curricula and on instructional materials and equipment that could be used as weapons. There is no Internet access. Sometimes, educational programs require access to security-intensive correctional information or locations: this access must be approved in advance by prison officials. Adult inmate movement and multiple other facts of prison life determine the availability of instructional time and locations.

Additionally, school leaders must ensure that the most qualified teachers are assigned to teach core academic courses, even for the most difficult-to-staff teaching assignments and in the most challenging correctional facilities. At the same time, jail and prison school programs must comply with state laws and regulations that mandate the number of instructional hours and the educational services to be provided. A structured, well-coordinated plan for juvenile correctional education and a firm commitment from the prison's executive management can improve the outcomes and chances of successes for school-age youths in adult correctional facilities.

As cities and states increase the numbers and percentages of juvenile cases transferred to adult criminal courts, it is imperative that local governments that operate adult detention centers and correctional facilities coordinate their efforts with their local school district partners. It is also imperative that both groups do their best to avoid legal, logistical, and educational dilemmas so that the educational process can flourish in prison.

CHAPTER **6**

Teaching: An Extraordinary Responsibility

THE RESPONSIBILITY FOR providing educational services to school-age youths charged as adults and detained or sentenced in the Philadelphia Prison System belongs to the city's school district. According to FBI statistics, violent crimes and property crimes in Philadelphia have grown at a rate that exceeds the national average. In July 2007, the *CBS Evening News*, with Katie Couric as host, broadcast "Battle Line: Philadelphia," a two-part story about the city's crime crisis. According to criminology researchers and other experts, a toxic mix fuels Philadelphia's crime epidemic: easy access to guns, high dropout rates, high unemployment rates, drug abuse, increase in the crime rate among black males aged 15 to 24, declining teacher quality, multiple stress factors, hunger, a deficit of commitment by parents, failures of public systems, dysfunctional homes, illiteracy, an overwhelmed criminal justice system, federal budget cuts in urban law enforcement, mental health issues, and a resurgence in gang activity. Take your pick.

Participation of the Philadelphia school district in providing educational services within the prison system was established well over three decades ago. At that time, the school district provided educational support for incarcerated school-age youths, including assigning teachers and offering instructional support services. As the daily adult inmate population of the prison system and the number of correctional facilities increased, the school district's role also grew. Today, the prison system-based public school organization, now with much broader responsibilities, is known to both juvenile and adult inmates as Pennypack House School.

Pennypack House School conducts systemic reviews of instructional goals and assesses how well educational objectives for juvenile inmates are being met. It supports GED testing and a growing adult education sector in the city's six major correctional facilities. School admission is based on open enrollment of both adult inmates and juvenile inmates 17 years of age and younger.

During the time I led Pennypack House School, from 2004 through the 2008 school year, I enrolled more than 2000 school-age youths, a population that overwhelmed enrollment capacity and posed tremendous challenges for both the Philadelphia Prison

System and the school district. During my first year at the school, a powerful educational advocacy group, the Juvenile Law Center, pursued its long-standing complaint against the Philadelphia Prison System and the school district. They accused both organization of intentionally denying educational services to school-age youths. In no uncertain terms, the Juvenile Law Center attacked Pennypack House's efforts to run an instructional program as totally inadequate, asserting that the system had long-standing legal, logistical, and educational problems that were not being addressed. In the face of these charges, the school district took the position that its obligation was only to provide educational services, not to address concerns related to the facility, the educational space, or logistics. Those responsibilities, the district maintained, belonged to the prison system.

The Juvenile Law Center made the following specific assertions:

Legal Deficiencies

- Most male students at the House of Correction did not receive instruction for periods of up to eight months, violating state law.
- Many special education students did not receive special education services they were entitled to by law.

LOGISTICAL DEFICIENCIES

- The allocated educational space had a maximum capacity for only seventy-five students; on any given day, another forty-seven were prevented from participating in the classes and receiving an education, and there was no plan in place to increase capacity.

EDUCATIONAL DEFICIENCIES

- Instruction was not sufficient in core courses—literacy, mathematics, science, and social studies—to enable students to make normal academic progress.
- Textbooks, educational materials, and supplies were prohibited on the housing units, limiting extended learning opportunities and independent study.

On my instructional rounds, I identified many other legal, logistical, and educational problems.

- Special education students were spending their entire school days in a self-contained special education classroom.
- Teachers were teaching outside their certification areas.
- A Pennsylvania Department of Education audit found numerous special education violations

in regard to management of students' individualized education plans.

- There was only limited awareness among staff of any cooperative agreement between the school district and the prison system.
- The cyclical incarceration of school-age youths, with frequent and rapid transfers in and out, overwhelmed the school's capacity to manage enrollment.
- Space allocation and logistics for the education of school-age youths were severely limited by a sight-and-sound policy, which required their separation from adult inmates at all times and thereby made some potential classroom space unavailable.
- Students' educational levels demonstrated wide achievement gaps.
- Failing grades were routine.
- Female students were not receiving an equitable share of educational resources.
- Technology use by teachers and students ranged from very limited to none at all.
- Professional development opportunities for teachers did not address issues pertinent to correctional education or incarcerated youth.
- Procedures for earning credits, monitoring and documenting academic progress, obtaining student educational records, and creating transcripts were not kept up to date and did not

mesh with the cyclical nature of the school.

- Teachers did not have knowledge of the school district's core curriculum.
- The major course offerings were in remedial and basic math and remedial reading.
- Male students under quarantine and those assigned to punitive or administrative segregation, protective custody, and health or mental health units were not receiving educational services.
- Student engagement in classrooms was very low.
- The number of classrooms was inadequate.
- The Philadelphia Prison System's educational policies served as the only legal basis for setting the parameters and formalizing the procedures for the operation of inmate educational programs.
- There was an overuse of school suspensions and permanent school exclusions as methods for addressing problematic student behavior.

Since most incarcerated school-age youths had attended public schools (and been failed by them), Pennypack House School had to be different. Despite the conditions of prison, I felt that the school had to be the one place where students could feel their lives improving in an academic culture that was nurturing and organized around a strong commitment to their growth and learning.

I did not have a model for reorganizing Pennypack House School. The only strategy I had in mind was to reflect on my experiences at the Bensalem Youth Development Center and couple my reflections with my leadership experiences as a high school principal. I knew that the situation in Philadelphia was not unusual. Correctional facilities across the country, and in other countries as well, are in great disarray when it comes to deciding how to work with their incarcerated school-age youths.

California presents a glaring case in point. There, advocates for incarcerated youths urged judges and lawmakers to reform the entire juvenile justice system and appoint a receiver to take over a system they said was "tragically broken." The situation came about because the California Division of Juvenile Justice had neglected to institute reforms in six areas: education, safety, medical care, mental health, disabilities, and sex-offender treatment. There were reports of youths in restricted programs spending 20 hours or more in their cells each day, released for just one hour of school. This was nowhere near the required four hours a day. Students were often removed from classrooms for misbehaving. At one school inside a prison, 347 classes were canceled within a three-month period because of teacher absenteeism. Even in regular public school settings, studies link teacher absences to lower student achievement.

In 2000-2001, Maryland governor Parris N.

Glendening courageously spearheaded an investigation into conditions at the Baltimore City Detention Center. This investigation was one of the most comprehensive efforts for addressing juvenile correctional issues that I have seen. While much attention was paid to violations in the sight-and-sound policy and the isolation of some school-age youths in segregation cells for lengthy periods (causing some to suffer psychological damage), another issue was central to the inspection: the quality of education afforded school-age youths confined to the center.

The violations were extensive and disturbing. Among the many problems cited were the following:

- The public school inside the Baltimore City Detention Center had failed to identify and evaluate school-age youths who may have needed special education services.
- Girls were not provided with educational opportunities comparable to those of their male counterparts.
- School-age youths housed in maximum security were not receiving an education comparable to that of the general school population.
- There was no system of monitoring student progress in classrooms.
- Space and resources were inadequate or inappropriate to deliver effective and meaningful instruction to all students.

- The student enrollment system was inefficient and lagging.
- There was no focus or integration to the curriculum and it had no functional standards.

Philadelphia, California, and Baltimore are not unique. Pick any major city, state, or country and you will probably find some need for major systemic change in how incarcerated school-age youths are educated and how their academic skills are being developed. Everywhere, even as far away as Eastern Europe and countries of the former Soviet Union, the role of education in juvenile justice is being closely examined.

Every country faces issues related to incarceration of school-age youths. As a result, the demand for and importance of education for this population is growing steadily around the world. It is urgent that focus be placed on building educational structures, processes, and systems in correctional facilities to ensure that incarcerated children and youths receive more than just a lifetime of punishment for their actions.

In Eastern Europe, the Constitutional and Legal Policy Institute (COLPI), the legal reform support program of the Open Society Institute-Budapest, has made reforming juvenile justice systems in its constituent countries and the former Soviet Union a major priority. COLPI is steadfast in implementing criminal justice reforms, including the right to education

.

of incarcerated school-age youths. COLPI is raising provocative issues on educational policies concerning incarcerated school-age youths and lobbying for a comprehensive range of approaches and programs, without regard to gender.

In 2006, as a response to the long-standing legal, logistical, and educational dilemmas of the Philadelphia Prison System and in a dedicated effort to bring coherence to the education of incarcerated school-age youths charged as adults, I developed the Juvenile Focused Correctional Education School Model (JFCESM). Today, school-age youths benefit from processes and systems that focus directly on the instructional core and give them what they need to succeed academically.

The Juvenile Focused Correctional Education School Model embodies commitment to incarcerated school-age youths. More important, it provides a way to help students develop academic performance, confidence, the ability to handle stress, a sense of well-being, and the motivation to succeed. The next chapter presents the model in detail.

CHAPTER 7

The Juvenile Focused Correctional Education School Model and Its Results

THIS CHAPTER PRESENTS the model for focused correctional education for juveniles, a description of the initial implementation (in Philadelphia), and the results achieved by applying the model.

MISSION STATEMENT

THE MISSION STATEMENT is intentionally clear and concise. No complex educational jargon allowed! Incarcerated school-age youths must themselves understand the mission and its focus on the instructional core. In simple words:

Create an academic environment, in the adult correctional setting, that encourages school-aged youths to take advantage of academic and educational opportunities. In doing so, they will reconnect with public school, meet challenging state academic standards required of all students in the

Commonwealth of Pennsylvania, and achieve their educational pursuits.

General Approach

- Afford flexibility to change structures, features, and practices, while ensuring that the Philadelphia Prison System and School District of Philadelphia work together to address everyday issues affecting the students.
- Serve as the blueprint for building academic capacity, creating an academic culture, and promoting a correctional environment that leads students to academic growth and learning.
- Adapt to all types and designs of adult correctional facilities struggling to create an educational environment for school-age youths while operating within the parameters of structure and the need to separate adult and juvenile inmates, accommodating high-risk inmates, and addressing capacity and educational space limitations.

Primary Objectives

JFCESM PROVIDES STUDENTS with structured classrooms, varied educational delivery approaches, and academic progress monitoring in a wide variety of correctional settings. It focuses on the following objectives:

- To deliver standards-based instruction in each core content area.
- To improve students' basic educational skills.
- To elevate students' academic capabilities and attainment.
- To provide avenues and means for students to progress toward grade level, promotion, and graduation, when eligible.
- To improve students' overall attitudes about education and their potential for educational success.

Main Features

JFCESM CAN BE applied in single- or multi-site juvenile correctional facilities, large or small, and in adult facilities housing juvenile inmates, including those with special management units. It has this flexibility because it addresses a broad range of considerations.

- Academics-focused program aligned with the academic standards of both the School District of Philadelphia and the Commonwealth of Pennsylvania
- Academic Assistance Academy for special management populations

- Academic outreach to students assigned to health or mental health units
- Adaptability to correctional facilities of various types and designs
- Bi-weekly standards-driven lesson planning
- Cohort teaching partnerships
- Curriculum enrichment partnerships
- Cyclical enrollment management system
- Flexible scheduling
- Flexibility to innovate continuously to resolve legal, logistical, and educational dilemmas
- High expectations for juvenile inmates
- In-cell support for independent study
- Interdisciplinary teacher team collaboration
- Juvenile correctional education methodology
- Juvenile unit support team
- Literacy focus across the curriculum
- Mixed-ability, non-graded classrooms
- Single-gender education strategies

POPULATION

THE POPULATION IS school-age youths who have been charged directly as adults under Commonwealth of Pennsylvania Law (Act 33) for alleged commission of a serious offense and incarcerated in adult correctional facilities within the Philadelphia Prison System. Once tried and convicted, they face adult sentences, including life terms.

Grade Levels

THE MODEL IS non-graded. Each student is placed in a learning cohort and receives grade-appropriate instruction in core courses (literacy, mathematics, science, and social studies). The core courses are aligned with state academic standards and requirements for accumulating course credit. Instructional strategies are devised to meet individual students' academic strengths and deficiencies. Pre-testing with the Test of Adult Basic Education (TABE) is used to determine students' educational levels and individual needs in reading and math. Credits earned at previous schools are assessed and recognized.

Impact of the Model on Instruction

- Instruction is based on the assumption that each student can succeed and adjust to challenging academic standards and expectations. Multiple educational delivery approaches help reach students in a wide variety of correctional settings.

- Instruction confronts the reality of students' transfer to state correctional institutions. It also confronts the possible educational and economic disenfranchisement they may face after serving their sentences.

ORGANIZATION AND SCHEDULING

- Provides operational flexibility, opportunities for frequent collaborations and team teaching, manageable student-teacher ratios, and a small, harmonious, and cooperative learning environment.
- Provides schedule flexibility.
  - » 180 school days
  - » 4.5 hours of instruction per day (in compliance with Pennsylvania law)
  - » Extracurricular and advanced educational opportunities
  - » Opportunities for an extended school day and school year

CURRICULUM AND INSTRUCTION

A KEY ELEMENT of curriculum implementation is the effectiveness of the local school district's curriculum policy. The core curriculum of the school district is the principal document that guides JFCESM instruction and instructional planning. Adhering to the curriculum and its principles ensures that the prison educational program is coordinated with programs of the school-age youth's home school and enables each student to meet challenging academic standards.

Teachers use the core curriculum in the following ways:

- Guide course content coverage, organize instructional units and activities, and use appropriate assessment strategies.
- Adapt materials and approaches based on the core curriculum that recognize educational levels, security constraints, and cyclical enrollment.
- Apply principal's formal and informal feedback after instructional monitoring.
- Develop targets for instruction and learning to ensure success by addressing academic standards in each content area.
- Use assessment strategies that will allow comparison and monitoring of student achievement in relation to the core curriculum standards.

TECHNOLOGY

TECHNOLOGY IS INTEGRATED into core curricular areas, such as mobile labs, graphing calculators, academic software programs for increasing math and literacy skills, PowerPoint, and multimedia.

INITIAL IMPLEMENTATION

THE FIRST IMPLEMENTATION was supported by diverse stakeholders and a federal grant.

- Ten full-time teachers employed by the School District of Philadelphia.

- Faculty buy-in.
- Input from juvenile inmates.
- Support from the Philadelphia Prison System and assistance from its stakeholders.
- Professional development programs to train staff in the principles and components of JFCESM.
- Core curriculum, provided by the School District of Philadelphia.
- Title I, Part D federal grant for neglected and delinquent children.

RESULTS

THE PROGRAM HAD positive results for students, teachers and staff, and administrators and collaborating organizations.

For students

- Special education students received greater access to the core curriculum in regular classrooms, administrative and punitive segregated settings, and on special management units.
- A cyclical enrollment management system (CEMS) was developed to account for prison intake cycles and quarantined school enrollment, resulting in nearly 100 percent attendance.

- New resources and personnel changes enhanced academic programs and educational equity.
- Computers and academic software were integrated into the classrooms and made available to the housing units for in-cell independent study.
- Core course offerings were expanded.
- A variety of teaching options and approaches were expanded to enhance educational delivery.
- Students sought more assistance from the teachers and principal.
- Space generally set aside for adult inmates was acquired from the prison system for classrooms and small group instructional use.
- Use of the Pupil Progress Initiative (a student progress reporting document) improved student awareness about their performance.
- The use of technology tools and classroom libraries improved teaching and learning.

For teachers and staff
- Cohort design of teaching partnerships with team teaching enabled greater access and a more varied approach to the core curriculum and the strengthening of trusting relationships with students.
- A flexible school schedule was designed to balance requirements for instructional hours,

sight-and-sound requirements, in-prison movement, and other compelling penological factors.

- A daily common planning time for teachers and staff was established.

- New procedures for monitoring and reporting on student academic performance, obtaining and managing educational records, and providing academic records and other information to students and teachers were put in place.

- The school district's core curriculum and its companion resources for guiding instruction were put in place, and their use was monitored daily.

- School-based teacher leaders were appointed in each major content area to provide instructional support.

- A standards-driven format for lesson plans addressed academic standards, objectives, topics, materials, learning activities, assessments, pedagogy, differentiated instruction, data sources, technology, homework, and academic supports.

- Teachers received educational resources and participated in professional development to learn to use the model.

- Individual student report card distribution and conferences allowed teachers to measure and monitor the academic progress and performance of each student on a quarterly basis.

For administrators and collaborating organizations

- Compliance with state special education requirements and verifications and with the correctional facilities compliance plan was achieved.
- A new School District of Philadelphia - Philadelphia Prison System Partnership was created to increase awareness and understanding of Pennypack House School.
- School district officials increased their visits to the school and supported improvements in monitoring, communication, and coordination of school and prison education system efforts.
- Budgets were reprioritized to support resource updates, additional technology, interventions, accelerated learning initiatives, smaller student-teacher ratios, and elementary/middle-level resources.
- School leadership staff and capacity was increased, allowing school leaders to advise prison system officials on educational operations, program direction and development, system-wide educational planning, and policy development.
- Coordination with the Juvenile Unit support team was increased.

- Complaints from legal and advocacy groups disappeared.

- The cyclical enrollment management system (CEMS) process, designed and implemented by my administrative assistant, improved information flow and the integrity of enrollment information and management.

- CEMS influenced student accounting procedures in other local school districts, leading them to identify unclaimed students in surrounding county prisons and to correlate the coursework of students receiving public school instruction in county prison systems with those at non-prison public schools.

- Annual adjustments and personnel changes have improved the effectiveness of the juvenile correctional education philosophy.

- A document titled *Planning and Action Document for Neglected and Delinquent Youth* was developed by me; it links the prison school's educational plan and performance measures to the school district's strategic and academic plans.

- The quality and effectiveness of the juvenile correctional education program was recognized by the Pennsylvania Department of Education and School District of Philadelphia.

Pennypack House School is a model for success.

I believe the capacity solutions created in the reform of Pennypack House School will work in other adult correctional facilities that house school-age youths. Pennypack House School is thriving today, under the leadership of its current principal and school community. The reform effort benefited from extraordinary resourcefulness and support on the part of the entire Philadelphia Prison System community. Collaboration between the school and stakeholders, such as teachers, social workers, correctional officers, the prison commissioner, and others helped to facilitate a total educational environment. As a result, we made significant improvements in the model and the way in which we executed the vision, organized a school in a prison, and overcame long-standing legal, logistical, and educational dilemmas.

CHAPTER **8**

Does Education Belong in Prisons?

THE COALITION FOR Juvenile Justice reports that high school dropouts are three times more likely to be arrested than people who continue to graduation. In his *Education Week* article titled "Education Beats Incarceration" (March 25, 2008), Tom Carroll, president of the educational advocacy organization National Commission on Teaching and America's Future, states, "In study after study, we have seen that education investments that improve school performance and increase graduation rates can reduce rates of incarceration."

Even so, a basic question about the education of incarcerated youth must be addressed: If school-age youths drop out of school and travel a path leading to crime and incarceration, should they still receive our educational investment, even within a prison? With the number of school-age youths being arrested and thrown into prison nationwide increasing rapidly, it is clear that incarcerating school-age youths will not only contribute heavily to the operational cost the nation's correctional facilities in the short run but also require a costly continuing focus on their education.

According to the *Juvenile Offenders and Victims: 2006 National Report* published by the U.S. Office of Juvenile Justice and Delinquency Prevention, there was a 208 percent increase between 1990 and 2004 in the number of youths under age 18 serving time in adult jails on any given day. According to the National Center for Juvenile Justice and even more alarming, every day more than 21,000 youths are confined in adult correction facilities. In most states it is legal for children as young as 12 to be treated as adults. Under the laws of 22 states and the District of Columbia, children as young as *seven* could be prosecuted and tried in adult court! The national passion for punishing and sentencing children and youths to decades or even life in prison is an outrage; it appears eminently reasonable under the circumstances to expect that a system of education be awaiting these young people when they arrive at a correctional facility.

Some of our nation's largest cities continue trying to combat youth crime by attacking it on the front end, through early prevention and intervention efforts. This raises another question: What is the best way to spend taxpayers' money to address youth crime? Are these efforts working? The jury is out! I believe that cities should seriously consider developing the possibilities of public education in the correctional setting to reach the school-age youths they couldn't reach before they were incarcerated. So often we hear rhetoric about education from public officials: "All children deserve a quality education"; "All students can learn"; or (famously) "No Child Left Behind." If these statements have any truth, no student should receive an inferior education simply because of where he or she attends school.

Politicians seem to enjoy gaining capital by getting tough on crime and supporting efforts to build new, twenty-first century prisons, many of them for inmates who have dropped out of school. Just maybe, a quality public education in prisons would help those politicians and also be an important strategy for promoting student reengagement and progress toward graduation.

Every day, school-age youths arrive at prisons. Are we concerned? Are we ready to challenge our public education system to create instructional approaches and educational models that could aide in balancing the realities of incarceration and education?

In the United States, it will take the President and Congress to recognize that forward thinking coupled with legislation is required to expand and strengthen juvenile correctional education, especially for school-age youths incarcerated in adult correctional facilities. I put forth the following as a path for bringing juvenile correctional education reform to where it should be.

- Establish a national task force to examine issues in juvenile correctional education within adult correctional facilities.

- Provide competitive financial grants to school districts or correctional schools engaged in reforming education for incarcerated school-age youths.

- Establish objectives for recruiting and retaining highly qualified teachers in correctional settings.

- Improve curriculum development and implementation support for educational services delivered to school-age youths in adult correctional facilities.

- Identify solutions and accountability standards tailored to capture the performance and accomplishments of correctional schools toward their academic goals.

- Support greater access to technology and Internet resources in correctional education.

- Expand correctional education policy research and data collection.

CHAPTER **9**

What Makes an Excellent (Correctional) Teacher?

BEING A TEACHER is a great responsibility, and being a teacher in a correctional environment is an even greater one. A well-defined personality, confidence in one's knowledge of what to do, and not having fear of the inmates are essential to working as an educator in a prison system.

Incarcerated people, including young people, come from many backgrounds. Some have not been taught how to speak to others; some will make crude remarks. The teacher must have control of the classroom, and that control comes from engaging lessons and much encouragement. Many incarcerated school-age youths have not had good instruction in the past. When they find a teacher really wants to teach them, their attitudes change and they become serious about learning and look forward to it.

Certain qualities and strengths are necessary to work comfortably in a correctional environment and focus on what a good teacher is expected to do: produce an educated individual. The following list identifies some "must-have" characteristics of an excellent correctional educator. It is not a short list!

- Be self-sufficient.
- Be comfortable with people of all ethnic groups and social backgrounds.
- Build trusting relationships with students.
- Be an advocate for students.
- Be committed to educating all students.
- Trust that the prison staff will do their jobs.
- Articulate classroom expectations.
- Have educational expertise and knowledge of the core content.
- Be flexible and ready to interact with students constantly.
- Communicate with colleagues to solve student classroom problems.
- Realize when a student is anxious, frustrated, or needs to address personal concerns.
- Be respectful at all times, even in the face of difficulty or disorder.
- Insist that students be respectful.
- Treat students as you want them to treat you. When necessary, treat them as you would your own children.
- Be willing to correct inappropriate language or behavior and remind students of expectations.

- Do not be afraid of students.
- Never get in a student's face to get your point across.
- Place academics above everything else.
- Encourage personal growth of students, even in the most tragic of circumstances.
- Use differentiated instruction to meet the various educational needs of students.
- Be aware of each student's educational plan and be capable of helping him or her to meet its instructional goals.
- Be willing to seek the advice and assistance of colleagues to help individual students.
- Provide and direct individual projects that reinforce ideas taught in the classroom.
- Recognize that students are at various educational levels and require small-group and individual instruction.
- Understand that events that occur in the housing area may provoke changes in students' attitudes.
- Recognize that students may feel particularly stressed around the time they are called to go to court.
- Recognize that students are often upset in anticipation of turning 18 and making a move to adult status and being transferred to the adult inmate population.
- Believe in your ability to teach and do so as though your very life depended on it.

- Be open at all times to suggestions from students that could help the classroom run more fluidly.
- Communicate the importance of education and its purpose and benefits in multiple ways.
- Use your knowledge of the world to engage students in the process of learning.
- Be ready, willing, and able to teach, regardless of student attitudes.
- Be patient and compassionate.
- Assert yourself as the teacher and command your classroom.
- When giving instructions, be direct and explicit.
- Remain professional at all times.
- Apologize when you are wrong.

Correctional education requires courage, tolerance, and knowledge of the world. One must know oneself to be comfortable in an environment that may seem repressive and at times dangerous. You are a living example—someone who performs your duty and believes firmly in education in a correctional setting. When inmate learners are shown respect, given explicit directions, encouraged to learn and improve themselves, they come to believe that they can—and they do!

About the Author

HILDERBRAND PELZER III is a national award-winning educator with more than twenty years of experience in the field. His work as a teacher, principal, adjunct professor, and assistant regional superintendent has affected positively the lives of thousands of students. He has a strong commitment to boosting student achievement and improving learning environments.

Pelzer has been recognized internationally for his work in education, with special praise from Prince Andrew, Duke of York, for his school leadership. In 2008, Pelzer received the Queen Smith Award, which is presented by the Council of the Great City Schools (a consortium of sixty-six large urban public school districts) and Macmillan/McGraw-Hill Publishing Company. The award is presented annually to an educator who has made significant contributions to urban education and the community.

Pelzer's educational counsel and leadership have

been sought by media outlets, legislative committees, government agencies, civic groups, and educational organizations. Already well known for his educational work in the School District of Philadelphia, Pelzer went on to receive national recognition for his dynamic leadership of the Pennypack House School, the Philadelphia public school that operates within the Philadelphia Prison System—the fifth-largest urban county jail system in the United States. In that position, he directed the School District of Philadelphia's participation in the prison system and created the Juvenile Focused Correctional Education School Model (JFCESM), which brought coherence and capacity solutions to the public education organization serving the school district's incarcerated school-age youths. That initiative earned the school national attention as a model of success in correctional education.

In 2003, Pelzer established the Academic Renovation Symposium Series to bring together representatives of public high schools, community organizations, clergy, media, and legislative bodies to discuss ideas and strategies for improving academic achievement in Philadelphia's neighborhood high schools. The symposium focused on ways to revitalize neighborhood high schools to help them reach their greatest potential.

Hildebrand Pelzer III holds a B.S. in Physical Education from Hampton University; an M.Ed. in Educational Administration from Cheyney University, and a Superintendent's letter of Eligibility from Saint

Joseph's University. He has completed the Harvard Institute for School Leadership: Leadership for Large-Scale Improvement Program at the Harvard Graduate School of Education. He and his wife Eileen are the proud parents of a daughter, Toni.

CONTACT INFORMATION FOR EDUCATIONAL SERVICES

HILDERBRAND PELZER III is available as a commentator, speaker, and consultant on education topics, including the following:

- Making a Commitment to Urban Education
- Juvenile Focused Correctional Education School Model Implementation
- Modeling Success After a School that Looks and Feels Like a Prison
- Unlocking Potential

Visit the author's website at:
www.hp3-unlockingpotential.com

CPSIA information can be obtained
at www.ICGtesting.com
Printed in the USA
LVOW13s0210301117
558129LV00024B/1205/P